Luther

D1149368

LANCASTER PAMPHLETS

Luther

Michael Mullett

METHUEN · LONDON

First published in 1986 by
Methuen & Co. Ltd
11 New Fetter Lane
London EC4P 4EE

© *1986 Michael Mullett*

Typeset in Great Britain by
Scarborough Typesetting Services
and printed by
Richard Clay (The Chaucer Press)
Bungay, Suffolk

British Library Cataloguing in Publication Data

Mullett, Michael A.
Luther. – (Lancaster pamphlets)
1. Luther, Martin, 1483–1546
2. Reformation
I. Title   II. Series
270.6' 092' 4   BR334.2

ISBN 0–416–00362–1

Contents

For Gerard and James

Foreword

Lancaster Pamphlets offer concise and up-to-date accounts of major historical topics, primarily for the help of students preparing for Advanced Level examinations, though they should also be of value to those pursuing introductory courses in universities and other institutions of higher education. They do not rely on prior textbook knowledge. Without being all-embracing, their aims are to bring some of the central themes or problems confronting students and teachers into sharper focus than the textbook writer can hope to do; to provide the reader with some of the results of recent research which the textbook may not embody; and to stimulate thought about the whole interpretation of the topic under discussion.

At the end of this pamphlet is a list of the recent or fairly recent works that the writer considers most relevant to the subject.

Luther

Introduction

We need first to establish the importance of the Protestant Reformation of the sixteenth century. Today the effects of the Reformation might not be thought very obvious. However, some historians have put forward the view that the Reformation set up new ways of thinking about man and God, new ways of thought that resulted eventually in modern capitalism and democracy. For the country in which the Protestant Reformation broke out – Germany – the Reformation brought religious disunity which helped to perpetuate the political divisions of the country until the nineteenth century. In Europe at large the Reformation contributed to three great conflicts in the early modern period: the French Wars of Religion from the 1560s to the 1590s; the Revolt of the Netherlands from Spain, lasting from the 1560s to the 1640s; and the Thirty Years' War, from 1618 to 1648. As well as generating conflict among Europeans, the Reformation is thought by some to have encouraged scientific discovery in early modern Europe, while others claim that it helped to foster the 'witch craze' of the sixteenth and seventeenth centuries. Clearly, the Protestant Reformation must be seen as one of the most momentous events in European history.

Part of a movement of religious reform that also took in a Catholic and a 'Radical' Reformation, the Protestant Reformation can itself be sub-divided into Lutheran, Zwinglian and

1

Calvinist Reformations. The Lutheran Reformation erupted late in the second decade of the sixteenth century and from the mid-1520s onwards was officially adopted in many German cities and the more or less independent territories into which Germany was divided. Outside Germany, it was successfully transplanted into the Scandinavian lands making up modern Denmark, Finland, Iceland, Norway and Sweden. Alongside the German Lutheran Reformation, Ulrich Zwingli of Zürich in Switzerland launched in the early 1520s a Reformation that helped to make large parts of the Swiss Confederation Protestant. In nearby Geneva, from around 1540, the Frenchman John Calvin pioneered a model of Reformation that was widely admired and imitated, for example in France, the Netherlands, Scotland and England. The Zwinglian and Calvinist Reformations were allowed to take root partly because the Lutheran Reformation had already made a breakthrough, and had challenged the authority of the Catholic Church. We can say confidently that the Lutheran Reformation is first in importance and in time among the Protestant Reformations of the sixteenth century. The importance of Luther was particularly acknowledged by Calvin, who recognized Martin Luther as his foremost religious teacher. The Lutheran Reformation in Germany – the primary Protestant Reformation – is the concern of this pamphlet.

If we accept this primary importance of the Lutheran Reformation, we must next try to establish the importance of Martin Luther within the Reformation. Historians frequently ask questions about the precise role of individuals in historical processes. In the case of Martin Luther and the Lutheran Reformation, the position is confused by Luther's own diffidence, his modesty about his role. He would not even have called his Reformation 'Lutheran', but rather 'Evangelical', based, that is, on the Gospels. 'I did nothing . . . the Word did all', Luther wrote of his own contribution. Here Luther was concerned to stress the role of divine providence in the great events of his day. An historian, however, would emphasize the following factors in generating support for the Lutheran Reformation: the state of the Catholic Church in Germany and Europe in the early sixteenth century; the social and political condition of Germany; the work of colleagues of Luther, such as Philip Melanchthon; and the recently invented printing press, which allowed the maximum circulation of Luther's message. Taking all these factors into account, as we shall be doing, the historian would still have to acknowledge the extraordinary personal role of Martin Luther. In trying to minimize this role – 'the Word did all' – Luther added, 'I simply taught, preached, wrote . . .'. He omitted to add that what he taught was a powerful and readily understood concept of man's salvation; what he preached was preached with unique force, sincerity, simplicity and, often, vulgarity; what he wrote covers a substantial square footage of a modern library – over fifty sturdy volumes in the modern American edition of his works. It is right and proper to talk of the printing press, but the printing press came of age for the pen of Martin Luther. So we may conclude this introduction by saying that the term 'Lutheran Reformation' is a fitting recognition of the importance of the man to the movement. We shall turn next to look at the condition of religion and piety in late medieval Germany and Europe.

The Church and religion

At the head of the Catholic Church on earth, representing Christ to His flock, was the pope in Rome. The high point in the history of the papacy had come in the twelfth and early thirteenth centuries, and especially in the pontificate (papal reign) of Innocent III (1198–1216), when the papacy had directed an impetus for reform and renewal in the Catholic Church. That Church in the middle ages was a vast organization, theoretically including all the peoples of western Europe. The moral character of the Church was that of the Christian people who made it up, both saints and sinners. It was, indeed, almost always in need of reform which, for medieval people, meant returning to its original state immediately after its foundation by Christ and the Apostles. As long as the papacy supervised reform, much was done to keep the Church up to the mark; in particular, a remarkably successful attempt was made to imitate the life of Christ and the Apostles, especially their total poverty, through the foundation of the Order of St Francis under the direct patronage of Pope Innocent. However, from at least the end of the thirteenth century, we begin to see a weakening of the

3

moral fervour and reforming capacity of the popes. A long-term struggle between popes and lay rulers, always a theme in the history of the medieval papacy, continued along with an increasing obsession with Church law and with money.

Partly as a way out of the political problems of Rome and Italy, the papacy in 1309 moved its headquarters to Avignon, close to the influence of France. For much of the fourteenth century the popes lived there, in a French provincial town, not in the holy city of St Peter, Rome. An attempt in 1378 to return the popes to Rome simply resulted in a division – a Great Schism – in the papacy, with rival popes setting out to depose one another. This unedifying situation was tackled by a general council of the Catholic Church meeting at Constance in Germany in 1414. The council effectively dismissed the rival popes and in 1417 started a clean sheet with a new pope, Martin V. The prestige of the papacy, and with it of the whole Church, had suffered gravely in the scandal of the Schism. There had been bitter, but Catholic, criticism from the saintly Catherine of Siena; more dangerously, the crisis in the Church had created an audience for the damaging and heretical ideas of John Wyclif in England (d. 1384), and for the trenchant criticisms and reforming ideas of John Hus (d. 1415) in Bohemia (modern Czechoslovakia). With the ending of the Schism, the papacy regained some of its earlier prestige. However, a great deal of authority over the Church in the various national states had been stripped away from the Roman papacy and redistributed to national monarchs, especially those of France and England.

As the papacy lost some of its European influence, it tended to become more Italianized in its personnel and its interests. This meant that the popes of the fifteenth and early sixteenth centuries were more and more taken up with Italy's cultural and political concerns, at the expense of their pastoral care for the whole Church. The strongest strand in Italian cultural life of the fifteenth century was the movement of artistic and literary rediscovery that we know as the Renaissance. From the pontificate of Nicholas V (1447–55) onwards, popes became increasingly absorbed by their role as major sponsors of the artists and writers of the day. Since artistic patronage is expensive, popes increasingly used their command of the Church's spiritual resources to raise funds for the promotion of the arts through the sale of spiritual commodities. One instance of this tendency is of particular importance. From 1450 onwards popes were engaged in a long-term building project to replace the old basilica of St Peter in Rome with a splendid creation in the latest architectural tastes. The enterprise gobbled up money, and Pope Leo X (1513–21) adopted a complicated scheme to raise money by selling spiritual benefits, known as Indulgences, in Germany. As we shall see, the doctrinal implications of this sale aroused Luther's anger and set him on a collision course with the Church leadership, the outcome of which was the German Reformation. The spiritual exploitation and corruption which followed on the post-Schism papacy's full acceptance of a role as sponsor for the arts were important factors in serving to discredit it.

The papacy was not just involved in the leadership of the Italian Renaissance but also in the politics of the various separate states into which Italy was then divided. Pope Leo, and his brother and successor after a brief interval, Pope Clement VII (1523–34), came from the leading family in Florence, the Medici. Indeed, popes in this period tended to come from, or have strong links with, Italian ruling and aristocratic families and, just as the Medici popes thought constantly of the politics of Florence and Italy, so other popes used the papacy to advance the interests of their families within the Italian political system. For example, the pope when Luther was born, Sixtus IV (1471–84) waged war in Italy to promote the interests of his kindred. At the same time, the papacy itself governed a sizeable Italian territorial state – the Papal State – in central Italy, a state whose defence or expansion sometimes dominated the thinking of popes, even if they were not obsessed with their own families. Such concern with the interests of the Papal State could even extend to personal military activity on the part of a pope. Pope Julius II (1503–13) was the ultimate realization of the pope as politician and warrior, and his most unChristlike military exploits, in armour, aroused scandal and scorn in Christendom.

We should not exaggerate this sense of shock at the conduct of popes. The goings–on of the great ones were not as widely known then as they are now, and much that might have been disquieting was not known to the faithful. There was much latent respect for the office of the pope. At the start of his protest against the Church, Luther took issue with Indulgences, not with Pope Leo, and continued for some time addressing the pope with almost exaggerated respect. However, there may have been disappointment that the popes – vicars of Christ – were so unlike Christ. Many people were influenced by the body of medieval prophetic writing that looked to an 'angelic pope' to lead the Church. Clearly, popes such as the blatantly immoral Alexander VI (1492–1502) and the militarist Julius II were far from 'angelic'. Above all, the varied interest of most of the popes of Luther's period – politics, the arts, their families, pleasure – prevented their giving any more than token attention to the many problems of the Church.

Catholic Church councils of the fifteenth century – those of Constance (1414–18) and Basel (1431–49) – had tried to clean up the corruption of the Church, by putting constitutional checks on the powers of the popes; in general they failed. In the course of the fourteenth and fifteenth centuries, in the rising national monarchies of western Europe, papal powers were increasingly devolved upon kings. The most important of these powers were those of appointment, especially the appointment of bishops, who often functioned as state servants. As for Germany, the country's formal relations with the papacy were regulated by the Concordat of Vienna of 1448, but, as we shall see, the country was politically fragmented, so the Concordat did little to limit papal abuses. Germans felt that their nation was drained of money in papal taxes and dues, that it was, as they put it, the 'milch-cow' of the papacy. Their grievances against the papacy were regularly set out in the lists of *gravamina* or complaints, presented by the country's federal assembly, the *Reichstag* or Diet. The sense of grievance against Rome was also expressed in the rich literature of complaint and reform preceding the Reformation. Examples of this literature are the anonymous *Reformation of the Emperor Sigismund* (1439) and *Vadiscus* by the imperial knight, Ulrich von Hutten (1518). The national mood of protest against the papal Church, fuelled by intense but frustrated nationalism, explains much of the German response to Martin Luther.

Was the Church in Germany corrupt? There were certainly flagrant abuses, one of the most shocking of which was trading on the credulity or anxiety of pious people so as to make money out of the display and veneration of relics (holy objects, pieces of the clothing, bodies, etc., of Christ and the saints). Most of these relics were spurious, such as hay from the manger of the child Jesus, the foreskin from His circumcision, thorns from the Crown of Thorns, the girdle and the mother's milk of Mary, and countless alleged pieces of the Cross of Christ. Martin Luther's ruler, the Elector of Saxony, was a great collector of relics, the veneration of which was supposed to convey spiritual benefits, especially remission of guilt for sins, called Indulgences. The relic trade also catered for people's sense of art, wonder and history: relics were kept in elaborately worked receptacles and the relic collections were museums and art galleries to visit, exhibiting such wonders as the rope Judas used to hang himself. The cult of relics shows the mingling of religion and a rich popular culture in pre-Reformation Germany. For purists, this fusion of piety and popular entertainment was itself corruption.

Corruption was also evident when the Catholic Church and its clergy set themselves superhuman standards and failed to live up to them. This was the case with the inability of many monks, friars and nuns to fulfil the demands of poverty, chastity and obedience to their rules and superiors. Despite, or because of, the ban on marriage for priests, many parish clergy lived with mistresses who were wives in all but name. It is significant that the Protestant Reformation, when it came, promptly called for a married clergy, Luther himself setting an example by his marriage to a former nun in 1525. The ban on clerical marriage, as it were creating a sin where none existed, gave rise to much guilt, concealment and hypocrisy; it also produced a regular income for some unscrupulous bishops who charged their priests dispensations for the 'sin' of keeping a consort. In addition, and also because of the ban on clerical marriage, many Germans thought the clergy uncommonly lustful. A popular verse proclaimed that a house could be pure only if priests and monks were kept out. Sexual suspicion of the clergy added to the currents of anti-clericalism, i.e. bitter hostility to the clergy, in pre-Reformation Germany.

7

The corruption of the Church should not be made too much of in our analysis of Luther and his protest. The corruption was there, certainly. But it was not at the centre of Luther's concern. He attacked a corruptly advertised Indulgence in 1517, one that was shamefully hawked around, preying on people's religious fears and making completely bogus claims. But in launching this attack, Luther was seizing the opportunity presented by the indefensible abuse of a particular practice to express his accumulating doubts about the theology of the Catholic Church on how a man could achieve salvation. As far as the Catholic Church was concerned, Indulgences – pardons for guilt still attaching to sins already forgiven (see pp. 27–8) – were part of an extensive apparatus by which the Church was commissioned to help souls heavenward. Pilgrimages, masses, sacraments such as Holy Communion and good deeds were some other parts of the interlinked equipment by which the Church helped the baptized, believing Christian, through using his limited freedom of choice, to co-operate with God in saving his soul from hell. Luther, on the other hand, probably between 1513 and the protest of 1517, had come to believe that Christians are saved by a much simpler route, by-passing many of the facilities of the Church and trusting only in the death of Christ to wash away their sins. By 1517 Luther was coming increasingly to disagree with his Church over the means of redemption. 'Corruption' for Luther was a secondary issue.

When the Catholic Church reformed itself in the sixteenth century it retained Indulgences, though purged of commercialism, as part of its salvationary armoury, because they fitted in with a basic Catholic philosophy of how Christians might be saved; but when Luther set out to create a new and purified church, he never for a moment considered retaining even reformed Indulgences: the just were saved by faith *alone*. Indeed, it is noteworthy that those contemporary reformists, such as the Dutch scholar Erasmus, who put abuses and corruption at the head of their agenda remained Catholic in the end, while Luther, who put doctrine before practice, broke away from a Church to whose practice he could not accommodate his theory. The reformists stayed Catholic, the reformers became Protestants. Yet, having put 'corruption' in its place, we must also recognize its role in giving Luther a following. Millions of Germans saw in him a uniquely eloquent and courageous critic of a diseased Church. In other words many, somewhat mistakenly, took Luther to be primarily a critic and reformer of existing abuses.

If, then, we were to dwell too much on the corruption of the Catholic Church at the end of the middle ages, we would miss the point of Luther and see him simply as a second Erasmus, no more than a critic of everyday abuses. In addition, too much concentration on these abuses will shut our eyes to the living springs of reform and renewal in the pre-Reformation German Church. After all, in his early years as a monk Luther clearly did not belong to a 'corrupt' monastery, nor was he a corrupt monk – far from it. His superior and spiritual adviser, Johann von Staupitz (1468/9–1525) was an active reformer of Luther's order, the Augustinians, as was also the fifteenth-century German Cardinal, Nicholas of Cusa (*c.* 1400–64) a reformer of monks and monasteries. The most successful monastic reforms in pre-Reformation Germany were those associated with the Augustinian Canons Regular at Windesheim and the Benedictines at Bursfeld.

Pious clergy shared with pious German lay folk a desire for the spiritual life. In the fourteenth century Germany had given to Christianity a school of mystics of whom the most brilliant was Meister Eckhart, writing in German for nuns and for lay people living in the world. Beginning in the fourteenth century, the 'new devotion' (*devotio moderna*) was promoted by the Brethren of the Common Life, groups of pious individuals working in the world and specializing in Christian school-teaching: their pupils included Erasmus. The *devotio moderna* originated in the Netherlands and its influence spread to nearby Germany, where the relatively high levels of literacy in cities like Nürnberg and Strassburg encouraged the reading of such religious classics as the *Imitation of Christ* by Thomas à Kempis (*c.* 1380–1471), an exponent of the *devotio moderna*. Above all, pious Germans before the Reformation were reading, or having read to them, the Bible, in German, in numerous editions, and in print.

The particular emphases of German, and indeed of late medieval European piety can be seen in some of the German artistic masterpieces of the period. One example is Matthäus Grünewald's

Isenheim Altarpiece(1503?), with its almost unbearably anguished portrayal of the Crucifixion. In this work the artist dwelt on the human agony of the Crucified, part of an appreciation of Jesus the man which emphasized the suffering, as well as the triumph, of His passion and death. Grünewald's *Altarpiece* had a musical parallel in a late medieval German hymn-sequence focusing on the parts of the suffering body of Christ, a sequence later developed by Bach in his *Passion Chorale*. This preoccupation with the passion and cross of Christ was fully reflected in Martin Luther's *theologia crucis*, his theology of the cross, a theology that insisted that Christians were saved only through Christ's Crucifixion.

This dwelling on Christ the sufferer indicated a deep interest in His humanity, an interest also catered for in a cult of His human family life. In the first place, there was the mother of God, Mary, whose emotional agony, as great as her son's physical torment, was captured in the *Isenheim Altarpiece*. For all his stress on Christ as sole saviour, Martin Luther never abandoned – indeed he encouraged – reverence for Mary. She was a kind of patroness of Germany, and especially of the country's poor and despairing. A work attributed to Michael Erhart, *Virgin of the Misericord*, dating from the 1480s, the decade of Luther's birth, shows the Madonna, a towering but infinitely compassionate figure, sheltering the ordinary citizens of a German city under her cloak. Mary's role as patroness of the helpless is seen in the remarkable incident of the Drummer of Niklashausen, in 1476, when a young popular musician claimed visions of Mary in which she outlined a programme of social renewal in which all, priests as well as nobles, would work in order to eat and all property would be equalized. Another, more strictly religious aspect of the Mary cult was the great popularity in fifteenth-century Germany of the chain of prayers focused on Mary and known as the Holy Rosary.

As part of the desire always to humanize Jesus and Mary, pious writers, preachers and artists gave them an extensive family. For Mary, parents were found, Joachim and Anne, and they immediately became the favourite saints of the German mining community; important mining settlements were named after them. To understand *why* German miners took St Anne as their patron saint would be to realize something of the richness, the complexity, the poetry and, for us, the strangeness of late medieval German popular piety. As mother of Mary, it was said, Anne nurtured in her womb a unique treasure; in just the same way, the copper and silver mines that the miners worked hid the rich treasure of their ores. As the son of a miner, Martin Luther knew he came under the protection of St Anne. When, in 1505, he was, as he believed, miraculously saved from a frightening thunderstorm, he repaid a vow to his saint that he would enter the monastery if she saved him.

The cult of saints Mary, Anne and Joachim was only part of a vast veneration of the saints in pre-Reformation Germany. Just as one needed powerful protectors in the temporal world, a dangerous and hostile place, so in the spiritual domain one needed one's patronal saint, perhaps the saint of one's parish church or the saint on whose feast-day one was born. The late fifteenth century saw in Germany an acceleration of the custom of giving saints' names to children. In Luther's case, it is clear from his early biographer Melanchthon that he was vague as to the year he was born, but certain of the hour and the date – the vigil of the feast of St Martin, in whose honour he was baptized the following day.

There are other features of popular religion in pre-Reformation Germany which we might consider. For example, there were the extraordinary pilgrimages like those in 1475 to the village of Wilsnack in Brandenburg where, it was believed, the sacred host of Christ in the Eucharist, in the form of bread, had actually bled. There was another highly popular form of religion, which was particularly prominent in German towns and cities, and this was the vogue for sermons, to satisfy which wealthy pious people set up trust funds to pay preachers. An outstanding example of the German urban preacher in the pre-Lutheran period was Geiler von Kaiserberg, the preacher of Strassburg (1445–1510). Though learned in his way, von Kaiserberg specialized in popularizing religion. The dogmatic content of his long and frequent sermons was perfectly orthodox, and he concentrated on speaking out against moral and social abuses. His style and approach were geared to his audiences of ordinary Strassburg citizens: he used in his sermons the traditional German proverbs or the new-minted ballads and the stories of journalists like his fellow Strassburger,

Sebastian Brant, author of the best-selling *Narrenschiff* (Ship of Fools, 1494). As with Brant, so with von Kaiserberg, a constant theme was the folly of the age, of a German state system and society much in need of reform.

Society and politics in pre-Reformation Germany

The first point to make about the German political system in this period is that some historians have exaggerated its disunity. It is true that the German *Reich* (Empire) was politically fragmented but so, to a greater or lesser degree, were all early modern European states. In Germany's case the vast size of the unit dictated some devolution of power. However, the *Reich* did have a number of common institutions, one of the most important of which was the *Reichstag* or Diet, a federal parliament. In addition, the political reform agitation of the pre-Lutheran period produced other national institutions such as the *Reichskammergericht* (Imperial Court of Justice) and *Reichsregiment* (Imperial Council). The political problem in pre-Reformation Germany was not fragment- ation, or fragmentation alone, but the mania for consent. Germany was not an authoritarian political organization, but one bound by law, custom, respect for rights. Thus, when it came to a common tax, people might pay it or not as they felt inclined. In the sixteenth century this lack of coercive authority was crucial in allowing the Lutheran Reformation to take hold. Considerable attention was devoted to improving national institutions and giving firmer institutional expression to the nation's strong patriotism. Much of this political reformism is associated with two fifteenth-century churchmen – Cardinal Nicholas of Cusa, already mentioned as a monastic reformer, and the German primate, the Archbishop of Mainz, Berthold von Henneberg (d. 1504).

The German *Reich* had a national constitution which reflected the absence of authoritarianism. Dating from 1356, this was the Golden Bull of the Emperor Charles IV, a document which recognized the enormous importance of that group of seven reg- ional rulers, the electors (three of them clerical, the rest lay) who chose Germany's overlord, the Emperor or *Kaiser*. In theory, the German Emperor was Europe's leading ruler. He was referred to

12

by titles – 'Semper Augustus', 'Caesar' – which reflected his parity with the rulers of ancient Rome, a link possessing vast prestige. In fact, the German Emperor was held to be even greater than the pagan Caesars, for he was a Christian. Indeed, he was considered to be the leader of all Christian rulers; he was the *Holy* Roman Emperor, singled out by God to rule, having special obligations for the protection and care of Christendom and the Church, sharing with the pope the highest spiritual responsibilities. If all this religious burden were not enough, a rising chorus of German nationalism looked to the emperors to restore Germany's heavily dented self-respect in a Europe where France seemed to grow from strength to strength while the *Reich* lurched from one humiliation to another. Many Germans even held out prophetic hopes about their emperors, especially those bearing the names of the most distinguished rulers of the *Reich* in the past, Frederick and Charles. Artists like Albrecht Dürer lavished their genius on elaborating the visual propaganda of the *Kaiser*. But individual emperors seldom lived up to the image or to the successes of the past: Frederick III (1452–93) was very far from repeating the glories of his predecessors of the same name; and the reign of the Emperor Charles V, though it had its triumphs, fell below the standards expected of a second Charlemagne. Disappointed in their hopes of an imperial leader of the *Reich*, many Germans after 1520 seemed to turn to Martin Luther to fulfil their hopes of a national regeneration.

Below the emperor were the territorial princes, led by the electors. These seven electors not only had the distinction of choosing the emperor, but the Golden Bull had also given them extensive powers to rule their lands, powers which were copied by other, lesser, German rulers below the electoral rank. The seven comprised the four secular rulers of Electoral Saxony, Brandenburg, the Rhine Palatinate and Bohemia, and also the three leading prince-prelates, the archbishops of Mainz, Trier and Cologne. The inclusion of the archbishops in the college of imperial electors was an apt expression of the exceptional political power of the Church in the *Reich*. In many parts of Germany, especially in the central Rhineland, the states ruled by bishops, both electors and non-electors, made up continuous blocks of ecclesiastical land. Between a quarter and a third of Germany was ruled in this way by the higher clergy. Those chosen for the rank of prince-bishop came from secular aristocratic families.

Below the electors, numbers of other territorial rulers, such as the Landgrave of Hesse, or the Dukes of Bavaria, Brunswick, Saxony and Württemberg, ruled sizeable states within the *Reich*. Other rulers, usually classed as counts, governed smaller entities, sometimes as small as the County of Lippe, which could easily be crossed on horseback in a day. The rulers of the territorial states, whether large or small, had a decisive role in the propagation of Lutheranism, through adopting the Lutheran Reformation and imposing it on their states. The political independence that these rulers had already acquired made it difficult to deflect them from any course of action they chose, in religion or any other matter. The authority of the princes within their principalities was being underwritten by the introduction, or 'reception' of Roman law. Although this law came into Germany in modernized form, its basis lay in the content of legal collections drawn up the best part of a thousand years before, and its principles, not surprisingly, were very different from those underpinning traditional German legal approaches. In particular, it emphasized authority, obedience and discipline. True, there were Roman law principles that stressed consent: 'What concerns everyone must have the approval of everyone.' But the university-trained Roman law graduates increasingly being taken into the employ of the regional princes dwelt on those aspects of Roman law that emphasized the autonomy and prerogatives of the territorial ruler: 'The prince's will has the force of law.' In the German Reformation period, especially in the 1520s, the question of law and its sources preoccupied Germany, with many, especially the peasants, seeking, perhaps in Luther's teachings, a doctrine of divine law that would uphold justice and provide a refuge from the dawning despotism of prince and landlord – often for many Germans the same person. It might be said in passing that in their discovery of the authority principle in Roman law, territorial princes and their advisers were not always so quick to apply it to the relations between an individual prince and *his* overlord, the emperor.

Two political groupings distinctive to the German scene liked to emphasize the direct links of loyalty binding them to the emperor. These were the imperial knights and the free cities. The German knights (*Reichsritter*) were a variant of a species – gentry and lesser nobility – found throughout Europe. Generally they held tiny estates, often hardly more than a castle; and they were being squeezed to death by the rising power of the territorial princes. Though the knights were supposed to subscribe to the old code of chivalry, some of them were little better than robber barons, preying on the urban merchants whose wealth they hated and envied. At their best, though, they were cultivated men of the German Renaissance, like Ulrich von Hutten, or romantic heroes, like Götz von Berlichingen and Florian Geyer, knights who played a part with the peasants in their great rising of 1525. The imperial knights saw themselves as the direct liegemen and vassals of the *Kaiser*. Both the main emperors of Luther's lifetime, Maximilian I (1493–1519) and Charles V (1519–56), took knightly values seriously, and yet failed to respond adequately to the imperial – national ideology of the knights. In the early 1520s the knights, with their inbuilt anti-clericalism and their nationalism, thought they saw in Luther, in his patriotism and his demands for the reform of the Church and the *Reich*, one of themselves. Though he was a peasant by birth, there was something knightly about Luther and his bold, brave, aggressive gestures; for a while, when the situation was dangerous for him in 1521–2, he was taken into hiding and actually posed as a knight, 'Junker Georg'. Therefore, when the German knights rose in rebellion (the Knights' War of 1522,) their anger directed against the ecclesiastical states, Luther was adopted, mistakenly as it turned out, as their religious tribune. Defeated in their rebellion, the *Reichsritter* dropped out of the German political system as an independent force.

There was no love lost between the knights and the cities of Germany. The knights generally regarded the burghers of the cities as predators and parasites, squalid middle-class money-lenders. Citizens tended to regard the average knight as a lazy, drunken and shiftless thug. However, the greater cities shared with the knights an admiration for the imperial – national ideal. Both knights and cities feared the stranglehold of the princely states and looked to the emperor to rescue them. There were, indeed, major cities such as Leipzig that were part and parcel of princely domains, and Germany's most populous city, Cologne, had at least nominal links with the prince-archbishopric. But Germany's most famous cities were free cities, otherwise known as 'imperial cities' (*Reichsstädte*) since they acknowledged no overlord but the emperor.

This group of about sixty-five imperial cities included the artistic, commerical and industrial centre, Nürnberg, the banking capital, Augsburg, the west German bastion, Strassburg, and others great and small. Between them the free cities concentrated much of the economic, political, creative and religious vitality of the *Reich* and were the most progressive force in the nation's life. Nürnberg is the imperial city of which we know most. Tiny by modern standards, with its population of about 20,000, it was minutely governed by a closed circle of patricians who took a keen interest in religion and whose regime included, even before the Reformation, control of the Church in the city. In the 1520s the imperial cities – their governing classes and their citizens – were generally drawn to the Reformation, and Nürnberg offers a good model of the process of adoption, which was gradual, taking account of the city's relations with the emperor, but decisive.

Outside the towns and cities, the majority of Germans lived in villages, on the land, tilling it with indefatigable labour and primitive technology. Many historians have tried to generalize about the conditions of the German peasant in the age of the Lutheran Reformation. Was the peasant well-off or starving? Was his standard of living getting better or worse? The answer is that few generalizations can be made. So many millions of Germans were peasants; the very term – *Bauer* – is so vague and covers so many sub-types; and conditions varied from region to region of the *Reich*. We can, however, make the following four generalizations. First, though earlier generations of peasants had benefited from scarcity of numbers following the Black Death of the mid-fourteenth century, numbers were now going up again, holdings were being split, and lords could once again exploit the peasants' excess numbers to drive hard bargains with them and impose fresh burdens. Second, almost regardless of economic conditions, many peasants were still

16

consigned to serfdom and felt the shame and inconvenience of this antiquated system which lowered their dignity and restricted their freedom – for instance, to marry how they chose. Third, the peasants clearly felt that their own village community ways of upholding justice and law were being invaded by lords' courts, often using the 'new' Roman law referred to on p. 14. Fourth, the peasants felt oppressed by a host of cash payments and dues, notably the tithe or 10 per cent levy on produce paid to the Church.

Though some peasants were not badly off, and some peasants employed other peasants, even the condition of the more affluent was gruelling and required an ever-watchful suspicion, especially towards landlords. If the peasant family was to maintain or improve its place in the world, unrelenting effort and perhaps a certain grimness were required. It was into a peasant family that *was* destined to improve its lot that Martin Luther was born.

Martin Luther: early years

Luther was born in November 1483 at Eisleben near Mansfeld in Thuringia in central Germany, politically part of the Electorate of Saxony, with which his mature life was to be tied up. As we have seen, his parents were peasants, and initially very poor ones too. Despite later attempts by admirers to give him a noble pedigree, Luther never made any bones about his peasant lineage: 'I am a peasant's son; my father, grandfather, forefathers have all been just peasants.' Elsewhere, though, Luther added, 'My father was a born miner.' In fact, Luther's father, Hans, was born into the caste of the peasantry, but since the family property could not support all the children, Hans looked for work as a copper miner, finishing up at Mansfeld. Gradually the 'poor miner' prospered and became a substantial mining industrialist, paying dues to the counts of Mansfeld and joining the local council. Clearly, everything that came to Hans Luther came through hard work. The mother, Margaretta, was also a hard-working woman – 'my mother carried all her firewood on her back' Luther reminisced later – and the atmosphere in the Luther home must have been one of stern application and a gritty determination to survive and succeed. The later portraits we have of Luther's parents, by Lucas

Cranach, show a pair of tough and hard-faced partners in a life of struggle. The Luther parents were also conventionally pious, Margaretta more so than her husband who seems to have shown some of the deep anti-clericalism of the German peasant. As a grown man, Luther was conventional in his attitude to his parents. He paid tribute to his father's hard work and ambition for his son – 'by his sweat he nourished me and made me what I am' – but the acknowledgement sounds as if it is to a benefactor rather than to a deeply loved father. In the Luther home life was, no doubt, too serious to be warmly affectionate. Indeed the parents, conscious of the need to overcome human inclinations, liberally applied the standards of strictness common in German homes at the time. If Martin looked to his mother for love, he got ferocious corporal punishment: 'my mother once beat me until the blood flowed, for having stolen a miserable nut.' As for his relations with his father, a stormy, unpredictable, dangerous character, they were tense and complex: 'my father once whipped me so severely that I fled from him and it was hard for him to win me back.'

One writer, the American psychoanalyst Erik Erikson, has made a great deal of these later reminiscences by the reformer about his childhood. In his *Young Man Luther*, Erikson 'analyses' Luther on the basis of these and other adult memories of childhood. Erikson shows that Luther's theology expresses a need to placate, to head off the anger of a stern, judicial God, and he goes on to argue that Luther unconsciously equated this God with his harshly punitive father. Understandably, perhaps, those many historians of Luther who are in basic sympathy with his religous outlook resent Erikson's apparent attempt to relegate Luther's theology to the outcome of a disturbed childhood. Historians have also pointed out that the childhood memories on which Erikson places so much reliance were dredged up, many years after the events in question, and perhaps coloured for the adoring dinner-table audience to whom Luther addressed his autobiographical recollections. In addition, it has been pointed out that if Luther was savagely beaten, so were most, or all German children of the age, in a systematic programme of child-abuse which was underpinned by religious teaching and was fully supported, in theory if not in practice, by Martin Luther himself. Subject to a storm of criticism, the Erikson thesis remains an exciting approach to Luther and written without excessive jargon.

We may be able to deduce two or three influences on Luther from his parents. Himself a kindly father, he may have reacted away from the undue strictness of his own parents. He certainly inherited his peasant parents' vitality, energy and enormous capacity for hard work, along with his father's outspokenness and forcefulness. The Luthers' unstinting efforts and relentless ambition had been directed at raising the family out of the squalid anonymity of the fields and mines, and turning future generations into dignified and respected professionals. Martin Luther obviously repaid with interest his father's wish for a distinguished son. He also took from his peasant–miner background a credulous superstition that never left him, a belief in elves, goblins, witches and rustic devils that was exceptional even in a superstitious age. Luther's abiding belief that natural phenomena were controlled constantly by supernatural forces influenced his life at crucial points, especially at the time of his entry into the monastery, which we shall consider soon.

Meanwhile, the educational influences included, as he recalled, the teaching of Scripture (it is of course a myth, sometimes fed by Luther himself, that the medieval Catholic Church did not provide this); learning the Church's hymns (Luther became a fine musician and hymn-writer); and schooling in Latin, the passport to all worldly success. Writers from the school of 'psychological history' might make much of the fact that Luther, in common with all other German children attending 'Latin school', was torn away from his 'mother tongue', humiliated and flogged if he spoke German. 'Beating, trembling, fear and wretchedness', recalled the older Luther, misty-eyed over the sad little boy that was himself half a century earlier. And it is true that, for all his mastery of Latin, German always remained his first choice. At the decisive Leipzig disputation of 1519 he cried out: 'Let me speak German, the people can't understand me.' He might have said that he could hardly, without German, understand himself. For all that, Latin was the indispensable primary key to his later career as theologian, international writer, teacher and translator, the career that took another step forward when after schooling in

Mansfeld, Magdeburg and Eisenach, Luther entered the University of Erfurt in 1501 at the age of eighteen.

Erfurt was one of a group of German universities founded in the later middle ages. When Luther embarked on the BA degree course he began with, to us perhaps, an arid diet including logic, dialectic, rhetoric, grammar, ethics, metaphysics and arithmetic. The scheme of study was held together by the still prevailing academic approach known as scholasticism. Scholasticism, a fusion of the philosophic techniques of the Greek philosopher Aristotle with Christian belief, was divided into two schools, Realism and Nominalism. Nominalism reigned supreme at Erfurt. Its greatest exponent had been the fourteenth-century English thinker, William of Occam; in Luther's day it was taught through the writings of a former Erfurt professor, Gabriel Biel, and at Erfurt Professor Trutvetter was its leading light. Nominalism stipulated that the names of the categories of things, for example 'humanity', were simply names (in Latin, *nomina*), and possessed no objective reality. This elimination of categories made it difficult to argue out positions. Nominalism, disputing the capacity of reason to arrive at sound conclusions, strongly emphasized other grounds of certainty, such as Scripture, the authority of the Church and the emotions. Having in his studies immersed himself in scholastic philosophy, Luther grew disenchanted with scholasticism. In this, as in his dismissal of reason – 'that harlot reason' – Luther actually showed the impact of the Nominalist approach upon him, for this was a philosophy in conflict with philosophy. His sense of the unbound majesty of God and his appreciation of the authority of Scripture as God's word also show Nominalism's influence on Luther.

The relative sterility that some see in late medieval scholasticism may also have played a part in the emergence of an alternative approach to truth, by-passing scholasticism altogether. This was humanism, a combing of the language and literature of the ancient Greek and Roman past for certainty and wisdom. Humanism grew up in Italy, but it had its dedicated disciples in Germany, among them Johannes Reuchlin (1455–1522), Ulrich von Hutten (1488–1523) and Luther's Erfurt friend, Crotus Rubeanus (1480–1545); the latter pair were the authors of the bitter satire on monks and scholastics, *Epistolae Obscurorum Virorum (Letters from Shady Characters)*, which first appeared in 1515. The captain of the German humanists was Erasmus, and he gave German–Netherlands, or northern humanism, its characteristic emphases: criticism of Church abuses; satire; cultivation of grammatical and literary scholarship, through purified Latin and through Greek, so as to come to the New Testament in its original language; study of early Church writers, such as saints Athanasius and Augustine; and contempt for the scholasticism of the middle ages.

Was Luther a humanist? He wrote that at Erfurt he never had enough time to read the pagan classics of poetry. But such writings were only one aspect of humanism. When we consider the relationship of Luther to humanism, we should consider it under the heading of an important variant of humanism, *Christian* humanism. Luther's interest in curriculum reform; his developing study of Greek and of Hebrew; his reading of saints Athanasius, Augustine and Paul; his repudiation of scholasticism; his admiration of Erasmus: all these things indicate that we can consider the developing Luther to have been at least associated with German Christian humanism.

A clash of wills or of intentions arose in Luther's early academic career. For Hans Luther, who paid his son's fees and 'grant', there was a practical, hard-headed peasant's interest in placing the promising son in a sound, well-paid, honourable profession – the law – that would ensure the boy's future well-being and his parents' old-age pension. For the son, who was serious-minded, pious and throughout his education exposed to all kinds of devout influences, the religious life beckoned. Earlier, I stressed the dramatic impact of a storm and a vow in directing Luther into the monastery. And indeed, the storm-vow was the vital final impetus; but Luther's progression into the cloister was assisted by more subterranean and slower-working factors, such as the deaths of fellow-students from plague in 1505, prompting in Luther's mind anxious thoughts of salvation and damnation. Luther took his BA in 1502, his MA in 1505; his father, proud and at the same time seeing now in his son a social superior, began addressing him with the elevated German pronoun, *Ihr*; Hans had every detail

21

worked out, even to investing more capital – lots of it – in a presentation copy of the *Corpus Juris*, the bible of Roman law whose mastery would guarantee any clever lad well-paid service with one of the territorial princes. Luther junior, though, felt he had a direct call from God to the life of a monk and, abandoning his law studies almost as soon as he had begun them, entered the monastery of the Augustinian Eremites at Erfurt on 16 July 1505. Whether or not, by this decison, Luther chose to obey God the Father so as to defy Hans the father, the old problems of the tense relationship between father and son began again: Hans abandoned the honorific *Ihr* and reverted to a dismissive *Du*, and when Luther was ordained priest in 1507 an apparent reconciliation was marred by the older man's reminder to his son of the commandment, 'honour thy father and thy mother'.

Once in the monastery and ordained, Luther had other problems besides the resentment of his earthly father. The efficient performance of the tasks and purposes of monasticism – prayer, contemplation, repentance, the search for spiritual perfection – eluded him. On the surface, all was well: his intellectual gifts were recognized; he started collecting more degrees, with a Bachelor's degree in biblical studies in 1509; and he began a promising career as a university lecturer, seconded from Erfurt to the Elector of Saxony's new university at Wittenberg. Under this surface of satisfying, if not tranquil work lay a persistent depression and spiritual crisis.

From monk to rebel, 1505–17

Luther's spiritual experiences, his problems and solutions, have to be seen as continuous processes. Himself a dramatic man, he saw his life as a series of dramatic conversions and turning points. But we have seen that the vow in the storm that drew him into the monastery was, in fact, the crystallization of a slower development; indeed, we can speculate that the unconscious function of the vow was to give him an overriding authority with which to overcome his father's objections. Accumulating anxieties about salvation, so typical of late medieval Europe, brought Luther into the monastery. Once in the monastery, there was no change in

Luther's spiritual state, rather a gradual but dangerous intensifica-
tion of spiritual anxieties. Luther entered a strict and already
reformed branch of a monastic order and tried to make himself a
model monk:

> I was a good monk and kept my order so strictly that I could
> claim that if ever a monk were able to reach heaven by monkish
> discipline I should have found my way there. All my fellows in
> the house, who knew me, would bear me out in this. For if it
> had continued much longer I would, what with vigils, prayers,
> readings and other such works, have done myself to death.

The problem was that 'such works' did not convince Luther
that he was on the right road to heaven, or at least away from hell.
The difficulty was theological but, exacerbated by the fastings and
self-punishments referred to, it became psychological as well. At
the same time, a psychological crisis, an anxiety neurosis about his
ultimate fate, cried out for a theological solution. Luther suffered
recurrently throughout his life, and acutely in early manhood,
from what he called *Anfechtung*, an anguished combination of
guilt and temptation. He was faced by the demands of *justitia Dei*,
the justice, or righteousness, of God. God was a judge and since
man, even without his personal sins, inherited a state of sin and a
predisposition to sin from Adam, God's justice convicted him.
Since man was at base a sinner, the very 'good works' that he
tried to do in obedience to God's law were tainted, self-interested
and corrupt, and God would hold them against the sinner, adding
to his condemnation. The theologians whom Luther followed
taught that man's salvation lay partly in his own hands through
good works, but through his initial view of the righteousness of
God, Luther came to believe that damnation not salvation would
be the result of his good works. His overpowering sense of his own
sinfulness impelled Luther into constant, but largely futile visits
to the Sacrament of Penance, or Confession, in which he could tell
his sins to a priest, acting on behalf of God, and have them forgiven. Yet Luther did not feel forgiven by God, but rather
convicted by Him. He did not lack wise and pastoral guides in the
monastery and in his order; in particular he received advice from

the reform-minded vicar general of the German province of the order, Johann von Staupitz (see p. 9) Staupitz, a revered religious teacher in such places as Nürnberg, recognized Luther's problems and his gifts, took him off menial duties in the monastery, shrewdly told him that 'God was not angry with him, but he with God' and, finally, put him on a course of reading that culminated in a deep, slow study of Scripture. There, in the letters of St Paul, Luther at last found the way out of his difficulties.

The solution could be reduced, as Paul had reduced it, to a simple formula: 'The just are saved by faith.' There was no more need of the frenetic 'works' that only convicted the sinner by opening up the yawning gulf between his sin and God's righteousness. Instead, the righteousness of God could clothe the sinner in itself. Others, for example St Augustine, whom Luther, in common with many medieval men, read carefully, had approached or reached this insight. Luther addressed himself particularly to the problem of original sin, the latent, inherited sin with which man started out at birth, giving him an inherent tendency to commit sins of his own. Luther discovered that this sin from outside the individual – 'imputed' to him – was wiped away by God who likewise credited or imputed to the sinner the righteousness of Christ, who had died 'so that sins might be forgiven'. Man simply had to make a personal response, called 'faith'. 'Since we are justified by faith, we have peace with God through out lord Jesus Christ' as Luther's mentor, St Paul, had written in his Letter to the Romans. 'Peace with God'! Given his psycho-theological difficulties, it is not surprising that Luther seized on this formula of peace and trust, and that he even reinforced it be adding an 'alone': 'by faith alone' (*durch Glauben allein*, *sola fide*).

Just when Luther made this key discovery – some time between 1513 and 1519 – is a matter of some debate. In its main outlines – as a study of Luther's lectures in the second decade of the sixteenth century indicates – the 'discovery' was formed in time for Luther's protest against the Indulgence in 1517. Such Indulgences were based on a theory of salvation that violated the insight that Martin Luther had gained, or was gaining, that the sinner is saved by nothing else on his part but faith.

In the period betwen his entry into the monastery and his decisive protest against Indulgences in 1517, Luther was working out his theology. Indeed, he continued to work out its details after his quarrel with the Church broke out. However, some of the main lines of Luther's theology of justification were certainly laid down by 1517, and the protest against Indulgences was made from the starting point of this theology. One reason for accepting that Luther arrived at a quite early, if rough and ready, solution to his problems is that, according to his own account, he could not have put up with those difficulties for very long: his anguish was so acute, he said, that if it had 'gone on for the tenth part of an hour . . . I would have perished utterly, and all my bones would have been reduced to ashes'. Clearly, this is another case of Luther's tendency to exaggerate, yet there is no doubting the severity of his depression, or the fact that, even after he had evolved a solution, his black moods returned to haunt him throughout his life.

Apart from theological formulae, Luther seems to have found some peace of mind by throwing himself into his work. Academically, he was moving away from his earlier grounding in philosophy towards theology and, what became his first love, Bible studies. He tried to learn Hebrew, the language of the Old Testament of the Bible, and later, Greek. His career as a monk-academic flourished. As we saw, he was seconded to the new University of Wittenberg as a lecturer in philosophy, and in the years after he took his doctorate of theology in 1511 he gave a series of lectures on books of the Bible – Psalms, St Paul's Letters to the Romans and the Galatians, and the Letter to the Hebrews.

The year 1510 was an important one in the evolving career of the young, intensely hard-working and highly gifted monk, for he was picked out for a mission to Rome on business for the Augustinian order. On the whole he was enthralled by Rome, and though he had some criticisms to make of the businesslike attitude of the Romans towards religion, those criticisms took a long time to sink in. We repeat: Luther was not centrally concerned with corruptions such as those he found in Rome, but with the corruption of doctrine. His later attacks on Roman abuses rested on his belief that the papacy corrupted faith before it corrupted practice. The Roman journey was Luther's only trip outside Germany, and one of his few visits outside his native Saxony. From 1521 he was officially an outlaw in Germany and spent most of his time in Wittenberg: a provincial with a European reputation. Luther's visit to Italy also gave him later opportunities to indulge in routine gibes against Italians which became part of his carefully cultivated image as the down-to-earth German.

Luther had obviously been marked out by his superiors in the Augustinian order as a young man with a bright future. More and more responsibilities were conferred on him – heavy and prestigious administrative tasks, plus preaching as much as four times a day in Wittenberg and, of course, his teaching and research. Partly through his supervision of research students, he was acquiring a reputation as the leader of the young radicals in the young University of Wittenberg. For Aristotle, the fountainhead of old-fashioned scholasticism, he was now showing nothing but contempt: 'Truly we have been led astray by Aristotle and his comments.' Luther's radicalism at this time was relative and academic, involving the repudiation of an intellectual system which had held sway in the middle ages but which was now widely regarded as obsolete. Indeed, though an accomplished master of philosophical theology, Luther had become convinced that it was futile. He put his trust instead in reading St Augustine and the Bible, especially St Paul: in 1516 he describes himself as essentially 'a lecturer on St Paul'. Luther turned away from scholastic approaches because they seemed merely human concoctions, taking man away from, not towards, God. To approach God needed the Scriptures.

Linked to this idea of a direct link to God through the Bible, Luther advocated a simple, intuitive approach. This he found in a little handbook which he initially published in 1516 with the title *German Theology*. This anonymous work, which Luther believed to have been written by the fourteenth-century mystic Johann Tauler, was indeed an outcrop of the long-standing German devotional tradition, whose best representative in Luther's own lifetime was his superior and guide, Staupitz. With such works as the *German Theology*, as well as his *Commentary on the Seven Penitential*

Psalms (1517) Luther, even before the Indulgence controversy, was acquiring a reputation as a teacher of devotion, rather like Staupitz. In his biblical interests, especially in the use he made of Erasmus's 1516 edition of the New Testament in Greek, Luther was aligned with the biblical humanists, though he was not identical with them and grew increasingly impatient with what he thought was Erasmus's human-centred theology. Likewise, though he admired and made use of such semi-mystical and devotional writings as the *German Theology*, he was not a mystic (i.e. a believer in direct union with God through contemplation). In writings of the devotional school such as the *Imitation of Christ*, there was a distinct lack of interest in theology. Luther, though a theologian, and one who believed that the Church must get its theology correct according to the Bible as the word of God, was exasperated with too much *theologizing*, too much speculation, too much hair-splitting. This gave him some sympathy with the kind of approach found in the *German Theology*: the work was a kind of anti-theology. But the school of thought of which the *German Theology* was a product loved stillness, passivity (in German *Gelassenheit*, a state of poised waiting). Luther was not still, never passive, always impatient. With his discovery of justification by faith he won a kind of assurance, but it was biblical, not mystical. It was certainly threatened by the Catholic Church's doctrine of Indulgences, and when Luther was confronted in a particularly startling way by the doctrine, he reacted with the only form of defence he knew: attack. Nor should we forget that before the fatal encounter of 1517, Luther had been operating as a pastor, preacher and confessor to the people of Wittenberg, so that when he spoke out as he did against the Indulgence in 1517, he was discharging his responsibility to advise the Christian people in the ways of salvation.

What were Indulgences, and how did they affect Luther's theology? Indulgences were tied in with the Catholic Church's sacrament of Confession, or Penance. In this rite, the individual told his sins periodically (at least once a year) to a priest who was empowered to absolve (remit) them, acting in lieu of Christ. However, even after the sins had been forgiven, their guilt still had to be cleansed. This could be done by performing various penances and good deeds in this life but ultimately, if guilt still remained at death, this residue would have to be cleared by spending time in a hell-like state or place, called Purgatory. No one but God knew how much guilt remained to individual souls, but the theologians reckoned that most people, not good enough for immediate entry into heaven but not evil enough for an eternity in hell, had to spend varying amounts of time in Purgatory. People worried about their own future stay in Purgatory, a hell with a terminus, and they worried also about the time their parents and others who had done good to them were spending there. The Church provided for these worries: there was so much good accumulated by Christ and the saints – a treasury of merit, of which the Church was the administrator – that, through Indulgences, Christians could draw on it to annihilate their unassuaged guilt. The doctrine of Indulgences was elaborated during the medieval Crusades when the Church gave out that those who died on Crusade would clear the guilt that would otherwise land them in Purgatory. Similarly, those who contributed to the Crusades, and indeed to any worthy enterprises, would likewise receive either what was popularly regarded as a partial remission of Purgatory time or a total ('plenary') remission. From the award of Indulgences in recognition of donations to the open sale of Indulgences was but a short step, and one that had been taken in practice before Luther came on the scene.

But before we come to consider the scandal of Indulgence sales, there is enough in the theology of Indulgences in itself to affront some of the attitudes that Luther was holding by 1517. First, there was the way the theory of Indulgences had been worked out. One could go so far as to say that this was a kind of construction by human theological effort (always claiming some biblical basis) that Luther had come to dismiss as so much ingenuity, even sophistry. Second, and linked to this, the Bible, which Luther was rapidly coming to see as the exclusive source of religious truth, gave at best oblique and insufficient Scriptural validation to Indulgences. Third, Indulgences, based on the idea that the Church had a commision to act as God's executor, might seem to diminish God, to tie Him down to a series of contracts and covenants, and thereby to make God's power over to the Church and pretend to curtail His sovereign freedom to act directly towards His people; this challenged Luther, and all those like him who were influenced by Nominalist perceptions of an absolutist God and by St Augustine's awareness of God's omnipotence: 'Let God be God' might have been the slogan of this school. Fourth, Indulgences, with their gradualist view of forgiveness, violated what became Luther's view that God, quite suddenly, clothed the sinner with a borrowed righteousness from Christ (though the Christian remained a 'justified sinner'). At whatever point we can say that Luther's theology became fully developed, Indulgences could always be used as a negative norm to say what that theology was: Indulgences were all that it was not; they destroyed the centrepiece of Luther's mature, Pauline interpretation of salvation, that man was saved by faith alone, without any gaining of such credits as Indulgences were imagined to be. Useless at best, at worst Indulgences were actually harmful if they created a sense of security that excluded living faith.

The doctrine of Indulgences, even in its purest form, was opposed to Luther's theology, while at the same time undoubtedly helping to clarify that theology. We may hypothesize that any practice based on 'works righteousness' would eventually have brought down Luther's condemnation, though Indulgences made a particularly vivid example. Likewise, surely *any* Indulgence would eventually have provoked Luther's attack, though a particular Indulgence, indefensible from *any* Christian viewpoint in the manner of its promotion, gave Luther the opportunity to question Indulgences, and through them eventually the theological preconceptions on which they rested.

The Indulgence that actually provoked Luther's outburst was preached by an unusually disreputable and effective salesman, Johann Tetzel, and was part of an eight-year sales-drive aimed at Germany which, for the purpose of the campaign, was divided into three zones. The thinking behind the programme was a mixture of cynicism, secrecy and commerical squalor involving the Vatican, the Primate of Germany, Archbishop Albert von Hohenzollern of Mainz, and the Fugger banking cartel of Augsburg. The proceeds were to go in part towards the construction of the new basilica of St Peter (mentioned on p. 5), a seemingly bottomless pit for money. Archbishop von Hohen-zollern's share was to go towards discharging a debt to the Fuggers which he had taken on so as to pay the papacy for an earlier dispensation to permit him, in defiance of the Church's own law, to take up the Archbishopric of Mainz while holding other major Church positions. But Luther knew none of this and, needless to say, his denunciation of the Tetzel Indulgence in October 1517 made no mention of the financial chicanery in the background.

Tetzel was forbidden to enter the realms of several German princes, among them Luther's overlord, Frederick (called the Wise) of Saxony, the deeply pious founder of Luther's University of Wittenberg. Nonetheless, Wittenbergers crossed the Elbe, in droves to buy all-too-well-advertised Indulgence. Luther's first reaction was that of a confessor whose people were being hood-winked, apparently with claims that the Indulgence would even wipe out the offence of a sexual assault against Mary. And his response was also that of a theologian who centred on the Cross of Christ and who heard that credulous Germans were being told that the papal coat of arms was more useful to salvation than the Cross of Christ. He drew up a list of 95 discussion points, or theses, on what he took to be the still open question of Indulg-ences. There has been some debate about whether he pinned these theses on the door of the Castle Church in Wittenberg. The ques-tion is not very important: after their production at the end of October 1517 the theses were soon printed, giving them a circula-tion infinitely greater than the population of the small town of Wittenberg. Suffice it to say that the Castle Church door *was* the official notice board of the university, and that nailing theses to doors was exactly Luther's kind of extrovert gesture. The theses are a theologian's work and, again, typical of Luther in being the impulsive, rather dashed-off outcome of years of careful thought. They are partly silly: for example, Luther asked (no. 29) whether all the souls in Purgatory actually *wanted* to be let out. But the 95 theses also contained at least allusions to Luther's 'alternative the-ology': papal pardons were not the way man is reconciled to God (no. 33); every truly repentant Christian already had from God full remission of guilt (no. 36). The theses also made repeated direct al-lusions to papal jurisdiction, for instance numbers 5, 6, 21, 26,

31, 33, 38, 50, 82. True, in many of these Luther was actually appealing to the pope's authority, to inform the pope of the abuses being committed in his name. The next question, then, was whether the papacy would or could respond to Martin Luther and reform the Church's practice in line with a theology derived from St Paul.

Luther and the papacy, 1517–20

The year 1518 was decisive in Luther's estrangement from the papacy and the Catholic Church. The 95 theses were indeed inspired by Luther's growing doubts about salvation through any kind of human effort, but tactically Luther had drawn attention to an abuse of Indulgence sales and had appealed to the pope, Leo X, and to the German Primate, Albert von Hohenzollern, to abolish the practice. The 95 theses were hastily written and there were contradictions in them with regard to the powers of the pope. Luther stated that papal pardons were useful only if people did not put their trust in them – a major attack on papal authority – but he also claimed that certain wrong beliefs about Indulgences did not represent actual papal teaching, and he called on the pope to exercise his powers to clean up abuses. His tone to the pope, and to his immediate German superior, Archbishop von Hohenzollern, was deeply respectful: 'most Blessed Father, I cast myself and all my possessions at your feet: raise me up or slay me, summon me hither or thither . . . I shall recognize your words as the words of Christ, . . .'; 'Very Reverend Father in Christ, and illustrious Lord . . . excellent Bishop and illustrious Prince, . . .'. Luther, normally respectful to superiors, was also conscious of the gulf between himself – 'a peasant and the son of a peasant' – and men of rank like Pope Leo and Archbishop Albert. But he was still at this stage trying to avoid a confrontation with his superiors, and was in fact trying to invoke papal authority in his case. Meanwhile, though, the papacy saw in his criticism of Indulgences an attack on its financial system and on its power over Christians to judge, forgive and give dispensations.

In the declining days of 1517 Tetzel, whose actions had first aroused the Indulgence controversy, was entrusted with delivering the counter-attack to Luther. Adopting the academic method of

Luther's 95 theses, Tetzel eventually composed 156 propositions. When they were printed, and brought to Wittenberg, the students – always Luther's staunchest supporters – burned them; but Tetzel's riposte, however cumbrously, really did clarify the issue – that of the powers of the pope, which Tetzel regarded as absolute. Luther also added to the clarification of the issue which, for him, was one of grace and faith. More clearly than in the 95 theses, Luther submitted 28 theological theses to a convention of the Augustinian order in spring 1518 which effectively eliminated Indulgences from a scheme of salvation by faith only: 'Grace says, "Believe on Him", and already all things are done.'

Thus Luther challenged Indulgences and papal authority in so far as they clashed with direct divine forgiveness through faith alone. And as he was questioning papal authority as the basis of Indulgences, Luther was being led inexorably to find alternative sources of authority in and for the Church. For a while he considered the authority of councils of the Church, an idea that had had much favour with reformist thinkers in the fourteenth and fifteenth centuries. Ultimately, though, he would put his trust in Scripture, where he found his theology of consolation in the first place. This confidence in the Bible comes out in the full explanation of the 95 theses which Luther published in August 1518, *Resolutions to the Debate on the Value of Indulgences*. In the course of 1518 the line-up of forces started to become clear: on Luther's side, the authority of Scripture and councils of the Church and, suffusing everything, a sense of renewal and of religious power taking over man's life; on the Church's side, the traditional authoritative theologians, such as Thomas Aquinas (d. 1274), the pope as final arbiter on earth and, underlying everything, a lack of imagination, of real spiritual understanding or fervour. Luther was still receiving support from his fellow Augustinians, but his foes in this period were invariably from the powerful Dominican order, the custodians of the theology of their greatest member, Aquinas. Tetzel was a Dominican whose writings Luther treated quite contemptuously. Another Dominican, the Aquinas scholar Silvester Prierias, wrote against Luther in his *Dialogus* of 1518. In this work, Prierias showed that Luther was wrong because he disagreed with Aquinas and heretical because he differed from the papacy, which Prierias believed was infallible, incapable of making a mistake in doctrine. Prierias's sharp attack pushed the debate an important step further and drew Luther ever closer to Scripture: Prierias's ideas, he wrote, were wrong because they were his 'own, that is laid down without Scripture . . .'.

Prierias's proof that Luther was a heretic made the issue no longer one of discussion, or a battle of the books, but an issue of the papacy's right and duty to root out heretics. The pope's efforts to get Luther to Rome to recant (i.e. to repudiate his doctrines) fell through because of the refusal of the Elector Frederick of Saxony to hand over to the pope for judgement one of his own subjects, who was also the best-known teacher at the Elector's university. (Frederick's family were also traditionally bitter rivals of the family of Archbishop von Hohenzollern.) Everyone – not least Luther – had in mind an incident of about a century before when the Czech 'heretic', John Hus, had been inveigled into leaving his native land only to end his days burned for heresy by a Church council meeting in a foreign country. If Luther was to have a disciplinary hearing, it must be on German ground. The papacy entrusted this task to yet another Dominican, the eminent Aquinas expert, Cardinal Cajetan, legate to Germany for the *Reichstag* in Augsburg in 1518. Luther's three interviews show, on the part of the protagonists, fundamentally opposed conceptions of Cajetan's task. Cajetan understood his duty to be that of getting a retraction from Luther or else arranging his arrest and departure for Rome to face a charge of heresy; Luther believed the Cardinal's role was that of giving him a fair hearing. The sessions were stormy. Cajetan, a natural authoritarian, shouted at Luther, who was inclined to back down and accept a formula of compromise. At the same time, though, Luther showed his mastery of the traditional theological system by using some tricky arguing techniques. But Luther, now more than ever before, took his stand on the Bible: he could not 'withdraw from most clear testimonies of Holy Scripture'.

Essentially, Luther had already assumed the position that, as we shall see, he was to adopt at the *Reichstag* at Worms in 1521: he was 'captive to the word of God', and could not retract scriptural doctrines. The interviews with Cajetan only brought the breach with the papacy closer. Indeed, Luther's aim of appealing from Cajetan to Pope Leo X was undermined by the papal bull of 9 November 1518, condemning the errors of 'certain monks' about Indulgences. Rome tried to back up this verdict by attempting, more forcefully than before, to arrest Luther, sending the nobleman Carl von Miltitz to this end. Luther's fate at the end of 1518 and the start of 1519 depended on his prince – and sole effective protector – the Elector Frederick. A pious man in the old-fashioned way (he almost certainly never met Martin Luther), Frederick was the most important power-broker in German politics in this last phase of the reign of the Emperor Maximilian. As we saw (p. 12), the German monarchy was an elective one and the dying Maximilian was trying before his death to secure the election of his grandson, Charles of Habsburg, as his successor. Frederick was central in these manoeuvres, which came to a head with the death of Maximilian in January 1519, for not only was he one of the seven electors but was himself a possible candidate, much respected by his fellow princes and the 'patriotic' choice. Indeed, as a political force in Europe, the papacy favoured Frederick as an alternative to Charles of Habsburg, who had already amassed enough power in Europe to form a threat to the papacy's freedom of action. The papacy set out to handle Frederick with great care in 1518–19; part of Miltitz's mission was to award him a papal decoration, and his right to protect his subjects – even from a trial in Rome – had, of course, to be respected. In these crucial months Luther was sheltered by his prince, whose right and ability to safeguard him could, in the political circumstances, hardly be questioned.

The key event in 1519 in the development of Luther's thinking, and especially in his developing rift with Rome, was the disputation at Leipzig between Luther, assisted by his university colleague, Andreas Carlstädt, and the Chancellor of the University of Ingolstadt, Johann Eck. Eck was an impressive debater for whom Luther had a high admiration. The debate arose out of an earlier argument between Eck and Carlstadt over free will. It was scheduled to take place in the other part of the Saxon lands, ducal Saxony, under the chairmanship of a cousin of Luther's prince, the conservative-minded Duke George. In his intensive preparation for the debate Luther undertook useful study, which helped to give further shape to his ideas on Church history and Church law. The debates followed the traditional medieval format: skilled oral duels, in Latin, stretched over several weeks. They turned into a spectator sport featuring two outstanding contestants, Eck, and Luther rather then Carlstadt. Instead of a discussion primarily on free will, or Indulgences, the Leipzig bout developed into an investigation of authority in the Church.

In the light of the 1518 papal condemnation, Luther was turning into a violently anti-papal thinker: 'that spoiler of the Bible and the Church, Rome, . . . the Pope, devoted to all the furies'. Luther's increasing rejection of papal authority, in fact, made more urgent the quest for a source of clear authority outside the individual. As we saw, Luther had earlier toyed with the idea of councils of the Church as its guiding authority. Now, in the Leipzig debate, Eck showed that councils of the Church faulted Luther. For instance, Eck examined the ideas both of Luther and of the fifteenth-century Czech dissident, Hus, and revealed that on many points they were the same, and yet the Council of Constance had condemned Hus to death by burning in 1415. It must have appeared that Eck was here showing his legendary debating skill, identifying Luther with Hus; to do that would surely be to win a propaganda coup because, after his execution, the memory of John Hus launched a Czech Reformation full of atrocities against Germans and Germany, in particular against the Saxon lands where Luther and Eck were even now meeting. Eck aimed to depict Luther as a heretic to the Church and a traitor to the *Reich*. Luther, however, boldly accepted the challenge. On many, if not most points, he said, Hus had been right and the council wrong. Could Church councils then, make mistakes? Yes they could, and so could popes, and there was no recourse but Scripture. Like Prierias before him, Eck had proved intellectually that Luther was a heretic, but there was and could be no prosecution for heresy, and the net results of the Leipzig debate, apart from leaving a sour taste in Luther's mouth, were to widen the breach with Rome and to give Luther a lifelong admiration for Hus and a comforting knowledge that he was not the first in his field.

In Luther's career, the most important years for the development of his thought were those from 1512 to 1520, and the most important years for the establishment of his reputation those from 1517 to 1521. Thus the years from 1517 to 1520 are of particular centrality, for they form a period when Luther was both completing his own ideas and carving out his fame. In 1519, as we have seen, he was decisively protected by Frederick the Wise, and this protection continued during the potentially dangerous period 1520-1. Whatever the other sources of his greatness, this factor in his preservation stands out – the sheltering of his development by his regional prince. This early role of the prince in defending Luther's Reformation from death in infancy anticipates the later influence, especially in the 1530s, of princely authorities in the expansion of the German Lutheran Reformation. In addition, in key writings of 1520 which we shall soon examine Luther stressed the religious role of rulers.

The effect on Luther's career of the main event of 1519 – the Leipzig debate – was carried over into 1520 by Eck's taking his case against Luther direct to Rome. While the case was being decided there, Luther himself contributed to his final alienation from the papacy by his writings; in the same writings he also established his standing as a national hero for Germans of all social classes and for all of those interested in religious and social reform. In the 1520s and 1530s Luther probably lost some of the widespread popularity he won in and around 1520: he himself became distrusted in some quarters, notably by the peasants, as we shall see, after their failed rising of 1525. Also, in the 1520s, 1530s and 1540s the Lutheran Reformation, as it became institutionalized under the guidance of individual territorial princes, tended to become more of a sectional and regional cause, though a widespread one. By contrast, in 1520, Luther seems to have been a unifying figure, inspiring but not dividing what would appear to have been – from reporters not friendly to Luther – the great majority of Germans. This height of fame and achievement was won largely by three of his writings in 1520. These thematically linked tracts, generally regarded as Luther's masterpieces, were no doubt intended to have the wide appeal they came to enjoy: they were Luther's call upon his fellow Germans for their support in his great struggle. They are, in order of appearance: *To the Christian Nobility of the German Nation concerning the Improvement of the Christian Estate; The Babylonian Captivity of the Church;* and *The Liberty of a Christian.*

In *To the Christian Nobility*, Luther appealed to the political authorities of the German *Reich*, from the emperor down, to take in hand the reformation of religion and society, including such matters as educational and social reform. He gives the state a special Christian dignity and role. *To the Christian Nobility* (along with the 1527 *Instruction of Visitors to Pastors*) is a blueprint for the later implementation of the Lutheran Reformation in individual German states. In the radical and bitter tract, *The Babylonian Captivity*, Martin Luther evolves a distinctive theory of the Church. The true Christian Church is invisible, its members known to God alone. They are all of them priests. There must be a visible Church, but one should not give too much importance to its institutions and powers. Above all, the Church should not try to exercise temporal authority – that belonged to the state. To make money, priests had replicated a lot of bogus sacraments, but there were only two real scriptural sacraments – Baptism and Communion – though Confession, purged of abuses, could be useful. Children should be baptized at birth. Holy Communion was not magic but the supper of the Lord in which He was really present (without elaborate formulae to explain this) to the believing Christian. This believing Christian, Luther explained in *The Liberty of a Christian*, despite being still a sinner, was bought and set free by Christ and not even an angel could lay a burden or an obligation on him – even though he might voluntarily subject himself to working for the good of others.

The writings of 1520 made the gulf between Luther and Rome ever wider, especially *The Babylonian Captivity*, at whose appearance the knowledgeable Erasmus exclaimed, 'the division is now beyond repair'. Despite the olive branch which Luther held out in dedicating *The Liberty of a Christian* to Pope Leo X, the fatal estrangement deepened as Rome prepared a bull (a solemn sealed document) of conditional excommunication against Luther, which he received in October 1520: *Exsurge Domine*. The appearance of the bull convinced Luther, as some medieval heretics had been convinced before him, that its author was the pinnacle of all evil, Antichrist. *Exsurge Domine* gave Luther sixty days to surrender and when the time was up, on 19 December, amid a kind of carnival got up by the students, Luther burned the papal bull as a sign of contempt and as revenge for the papal burning of his books.

Thus Martin Luther finally renounced his allegiance to Rome. In his first writing of 1520, he had appealed for aid to 'Caesar', meaning the Holy Roman Emperor. Many Germans were united behind Luther in a mood of grievance, reformism and heady excitement; this mood, which had not yet hardened out into the later rigid divisions of Germans into Lutherans and Catholics, was well captured by the imperial knight Ulrich von Hutten with his clarion call 'to all Germans' against the foreign, papal bull. Would it be possible for the ruler of the *Reich*, the Holy Roman Emperor, to put himself at the head of this consensus of 'all Germans', as Luther had called on him to do in *To the Christian Nobility?* The events of 1521 would provide the answer.

Luther and the Holy Roman Empire, 1521–5

In 1521 Martin Luther was thrown into the turbulent world of German politics. He met another novice in the field, the newly elected Emperor Charles V. Since 1516, Charles had been gradually inheriting territories and titles, and the acquisition of the German *Imperium*, in succession to his grandfather Maximilian, rounded off the essential outlines of his European *monarchia*, his empire. A young man, Charles had yet to acquire the mature political skill that experience brought. He was melancholic, hesitant and deeply conservative; he was also perhaps aware that he, or his advisers, had already given offence in one of his hereditary territories, Spain, by introducing ideas and personnel from another territory, the Netherlands. In 1520–1 we see Emperor Charles V, careful not to outrage his new German subjects, feeling his way towards a settlement of what was already the Lutheran problem, and doing so with sensitivity, caution and a proper regard for the Germans' insistence on due legal process. Public opinion in Charles's German lands was, reportedly, well disposed to Luther. Nine out of ten Germans supported Luther, said Cardinal Jerome Aleander, with perhaps only slight exaggeration, while the other one attacked the papacy. Even among those Germans who certainly did not go the whole way with Luther – for example, the basically conservative Duke George of Saxony – there was much sympathy for his brave defence of German rights against Roman abuses, as evidenced in *To the Christian Nobility*. As a writer of 'grievance literature', Luther had fellow-travellers among that majority of politically aware Germans who felt that the *Reich* was much put upon by a foreign, Italian-controlled Church. The German knights, with their leaders Franz von Sickingen and Ulrich von Hutten, were staunch upholders of that kind of nationalist outlook, and insisted that Germans accused of crimes should be tried in Germany, by Germans, according to German law. If, for example, Luther's books were to be destroyed, as Aleander urged, their author was at least entitled to a hearing. Charles V certainly had to take account of such views, but he was also shaped by his own inherited Catholic orthodoxy, the faith, as he put it, of the various royal houses of Spain, Austria and Burgundy. Amid a confusion of invitations issued, revoked and reissued, Charles sought to resolve the conflict between German sensitivity and Catholic faith by summoning Luther, through his protector Frederick the Wise, for an appearance before a German audience. The occasion was to be the *Reichstag* convened at Worms in February 1521.

In the weeks before Luther's arrival there, the host city of the *Reichstag* was the fulcrum of all Germany's tensions and grievances. There were scuffles involving the emperor's Spanish guards; these incidents might have reminded Charles, if he needed reminding, that, even had he any inclination to favour the Saxon dissident, he had other realms to think about, especially those making up Spain, a place of fiery, no-nonsense Catholic piety, a country that would find it hard to take a ruler who was soft on heretics. But whereas Spanish opinion upheld a rigid Catholicism, German national feeling acclaimed Luther, and he arrived at Worms on 16 April 1521 to a hero's welcome. His appearance before a sort of committee of the *Reichstag* was arranged for the next day and when Luther came before this august assembly he fluffed his lines. The questions put to him were straightforward enough: were the books on the table before him (already an impressive library) written by him, and if so would he recant their contents? But the latter question was in fact too stark, and Luther ducked it. Could he have time to reply? It seems puzzling that a professor used to debating should be thrown by a question, and historians have speculated about a kind of stage-fright in front of such an intimidating audience – he was, after all, a highly-strung man. On the other hand, by keeping the *Reichstag* waiting for an answer, Luther remained in control of the theatre of the situation, so perhaps it was not so much timidity as a deliberate delaying tactic that underlay Luther's strange behaviour at the initial hearing. And the delay produced an added bonus for, in the adjourned session, Luther got the chance to speak to the whole *Reichstag* not, as on 17 April, to a section.

On 18 April, in an electrically charged evening appearance, Luther was put the same questions as on the day before: are the books yours, will you renounce them? The answer was at first meandering and donnish: the books had to be classified into those that were evangelical and consensually Christian, those condemning the abuses of the papalists (this provoking a sharp 'No' from Emperor Charles), and those that, admittedly, did go too far in attacking particular persons. But then, in reply to a pressing question from the official responsible for handling the Church's case on the floor of the *Reichstag*, Luther produced one of the world's classics of epoch-making oratory – worth quoting at a little length:

> Unless I am convinced by Scripture and plain reason . . . my conscience is captive to the Word of God. I cannot and I will not recant anything, for to go against conscience is neither right nor safe. God help me. Amen.

Whether or not Luther added, 'Here I stand. I can do no other' or whether this was a reporter's insertion has been the subject of some discussion. In these matters, as over the nailing of the theses, we are free to believe that Luther would tend to select the more dramatic form of words, of gesture – as he did, for example, after his speech, when he raised his arm in the traditional salute of a knight winning a bout. Luther was particularly fond of these knightly gestures and, as we shall see, he would soon have ample opportunity to play the knight. In the meantime, his speech clarified the issue wonderfully and it remained only for Emperor Charles V, with almost equal force, to put the conservative viewpoint, to speak for tradition and the whole body of Christendom against novelty and the lone individual:

> I am descended from a long line of Christian emperors of this noble German nation . . . faithful to the death to the Church of Rome . . . I have resolved to follow in their steps. A single friar who goes counter to all Christianity for a thousand years must be wrong.

With his chivalric code of honour pledged to the safe conduct he had given, the emperor allowed Luther to travel home to Wittenberg, but the Edict of Worms, which the Emperor and a depleted *Reichstag* signed in May, made an outlaw of the 'friar'.

Once again, Luther's major protector came to his aid, quite slyly. By prearrangement, Luther was kidnapped on his way back from Worms and secreted away to the secluded electoral castle of the Wartburg, there to grow a beard and take on the persona of a mysterious knight – 'Junker Georg'. Scenery apart, the Wartburg seems to have been fairly appalling. There was, at first, nothing to do; a sense of anti-climax after the hectic events of the previous months and nervous exhaustion brought on the old depression, compounded by sleeplessness and a chronic constipation about whose symptoms Luther was distressingly informative. The Wartburg period points to a future in which Luther's role in the Reformation would be somewhat more passive: at the Wartburg, for the first time since 1517, he was not at the centre of events; many thought him dead. The initiative, as we shall see, fell into other hands. None the less, Luther's spell in the Wartburg did prove fruitful in that it launched him on a new literary career as a brilliant translator of the Bible into German, starting with the New Testament. There were other literary productions from the Wartburg, but soon Luther was called back from such endeavours to more active work. He was recalled by the disturbingly radical turn that the Reformation of religion had

41

taken in his own Wittenberg. For the succeeding years, his attention was increasingly taken up by the need, as he saw it, to put brakes on the process he had started.

In the period after his appearance at Worms, Luther often took up positions almost peculiar to himself, for his middle way in religious reform was sometimes hard for others to grasp. Towards the end of 1521, while Luther was still in the Wartburg, there were disturbing reports about religious revolution in Wittenberg. Some features of these changes, if not their speed, must have met with Luther's approval – for example, the distribution of the chalice as well as the bread to lay people in Holy Communion. But there was another side to the changes: rapidity, violence, coercion and inspirational preaching under Professor Carlstadt and a trio of charismatic 'prophets' from the Saxon town of Zwickau. Luther found these people, with their claim to have a direct link to God, worse than fraudulent. He was also disappointed that Philip Melanchthon, whom he had left tacitly in charge at Wittenberg, was indecisive at best. After a brief exploratory visit in December 1521, Luther resolved to respond to an invitation from the town council to return to Wittenberg and end the disorders, as he saw them. The role of the prince, Elector Frederick, in these moves is ambiguous: no doubt, Frederick wanted to slow down the over-accelerated Wittenberg Reformation, which was drawing potentially dangerous attention to his principality as a centre of revolution; but as a senior member of the *Reichstag*, he was bound by the Edict of Worms and was not supposed to allow liberty of movement to a man who had been outlawed by the *Reich* – and excommunicated by the Church. In the event, Frederick more or less left the decision to Luther, with a formal ban on returning which Luther ignored. Luther's correspondence with his ruler at this time shows a degree of insolence certainly unusual in communications between subject and prince in the sixteenth century. On his return to Wittenberg in March 1522, in a series of brilliant sermons and exploiting his extraordinary prestige, Luther almost single-handedly restored order: no more rampaging mobs of students forcing the pace of reform, no more charismatics, a stern rebuke for Melanchthon, and Carlstadt eventually being forced into exile. Reformation was to come to Wittenberg, of course, in the shape of a simplified service in German, more sermons, no private masses, Communion for the laity in the form of wine as well as bread (Catholicism used bread only for the laity), instruction through German catechisms and congregational hymns in German.

The confidence that Luther took from his successful encounter with the Wittenberg radicals in 1522 may have influenced his attitude to recognized authorities. This more assertive attitude extended to the teaching authorities of the Church, the early fathers like Jerome, and even Augustine, whom Luther now tended to disparage. Luther's new individualism also influenced his view of the constituted authorities of the state. As we have just seen, he communicated aggressively with his prince in 1522. This uneasy relationship may have been the outcome of Luther's generally negative view of political authorities at this time, a view in turn affected by current events. No German territorial state had yet declared itself Lutheran; the formal assembly of princes and estates, the *Reichstag* at Worms, held a verdict of outlawry over Luther's head, a hostility confirmed by the *Reichstag* meeting in 1522 at Nürnberg; and in one of his non-German domains, Brussels, the supreme ruler of the *Reich*, Emperor Charles, was responsible for the terrible burning of two of Luther's Belgian disciples in 1523. As if all these attacks from political authorities were not enough, he had become involved in an exceptionally violent (even for him) verbal battle with England's Henry VIII, who was as yet still a papal champion and writing against Luther's reduction in the number of the Sacraments. The outcome of Luther's phase of understandable disenchantment with state authorities, even before the Brussels burnings, was his work of 1523, *Concerning Temporal Authority. How Far Is It To Be Obeyed?* In this work Luther, while deferring to the traditional view of the proper authority of the state as a remedy for sin, set strict limits on that authority: '. . . it is not to stretch too widely and encroach upon God and His kingdom and realm . . . God . . . will allow no one to rule over the soul except Himself alone'. In an impassioned cry for Christian tolerance, Luther echoed the liberalism of his own *Liberty of a Christian*: 'If someone imposes a human law on the soul, to believe this or that as the imposer dictates, God's word is certainly not present there.' Around this time, Luther was using unrestrained language against state authorities, with talk of 'drunken and mad princes': 'in your secular government all you do is fleece and tax to maintain your own pride and splendour, until the poor common man can no longer sustain the burden. The sword is at your neck.'

Indeed it was. Even as these words, from Luther's 1525 *Exhortation to the Peace*, were being penned, the greatest popular insurrection in German history, the 1525 Peasant Revolt (or Peasant War) was gathering momentum. We saw something earlier (pp. 16–17) of the grievances of the German peasants; their tradition of insurgency was expressed through their underground organizations, the *Armer Konrad* and the *Bundschuh*. The frequent earlier German insurrections had been limited to particular areas, such as the Upper Rhine in the 1517 *Bundschuh* rising under Joss Fritz. But the Peasant Revolt of 1525 took in vast areas of Germany, especially in the south and centre; its extensiveness was made possible in part by the universal nature of the concepts which inspired it. It was no longer a matter merely of regional or local grievances; a far-reaching and potentially revolutionary concept of peasant freedom through 'God's law' – a law which could apply in all the diverse regions of the *Reich* – had already been formulated by the *Bundschuh* in the early sixteenth century. In the Peasant Revolt, this notion of a normative divine law, by which everything – tithes, forest customs, rents, labour services and so on – should be judged, was aligned by the Lutheran compiler of the most sophisticated and influential peasant manifesto, the Twelve Articles of Memmingen, with the 'Word of God', Luther's key concept. Albeit selectively, the Twelve Articles form an impressive presentation of some of Luther's attitudes and teachings, as he himself recognized in his *Exhortation to the Peace*. Article 1 of the Twelve Articles faithfully reproduced Luther's 1523 demand that congregations should elect their pastors, article 3 contained distinct echoes of *The Liberty of a Christian*, and the Conclusion adopted Luther's 1521 position that he would climb down only if convinced by the Word of God. What alienated Luther from the peasants was, above all, the violence – inevitable, no doubt – that they showed in 1525. Yet his anti-peasant tract of 1525 itself urged extreme violence; written when the peasant cause was at its height, but published when they were already on the run, *Against the Murdering, Thieving Hordes of Peasants* urged the authorities to earn everlasting reward by riding down the insurgents. The effect of this apparent betrayal on German peasant perceptions of Martin Luther can only be a matter of conjecture. In the sequel to *Against the Murdering Hordes*, his *Open Letter about the Harsh Booklet*, Luther, apart from some remarks about tyrannous lords, did not really relent from the view he had taken in the 'harsh booklet': the lords and princes were God's punishment on 'headstrong peasants', and 'an insurrectionist does not deserve to be answered with reason . . . one should answer such mouths with the fist'. Did Luther's 'safe' attitudes in 1525 make his Reformation acceptable to German princes and other rulers? In the years after 1525, large areas of Germany accepted the Lutheran Reformation in a formal and constitutional way.

Luther and the German Reformation, 1525–46

In late medieval Germany, even before the Reformation, local civic authorities often exercised considerable control over religion and the Church. This was the case, for instance, in the imperial city of Nürnberg, where the ruling council appointed clerics and supervised ecclesiastical revenues. In the 1520s, governing councils in many of the imperial cities, such as Nürnberg itself, Strassburg, Ulm, Constance and many others, authorized and regulated the introduction of the Reformation, though the initiative often tended to come from the common people. These ruling councils did not permit or introduce religious changes simply because they wanted to assume the Catholic Church's powers over appointments and finance in their localities: Nürnberg, as we have just seen, and another great centre of the German Reformation in the imperial cities, Strassburg, already had such powers exercised by the councils. Nor, on the other hand, did the ruling councils introduce the Reformation simply in response to popular agitation from below, or out of fear of the lower classes, though there was much popular clamour for change, as in places like Frankfurt-am-Main, and the ruling magistrates often had to take on the task of phasing in the Reformation gradually. We should never assume that the governors of the German cities, or of the princely territorial states either, were simply motivated by political and financial considerations in implementing religious reform – though it is true that, in the cities in particular, rulers were strongly influenced by the need to maintain peace and civic unity. But they were Germans of their age, not political calculating machines; they tended as such to be deeply pious, and frequently fired by religious enthusiasm for the 'Evangelical' (i.e. Lutheran) cause. One such individual was the single most decisive force in the introduction of the Reformation in Nürnberg, Lazarus Spengler, the council secretary. As for religious Reformation for the sake of political advantage, Nürnberg and its city fathers were not only traditionally pro-imperialist and pro-Habsburg, but they also had to consider the firmly Catholic religious attitudes of the Habsburg overlords of the *Reich*. In the crucial period of the Lutheran Reformation in Nürnberg, 1524–5, the ruling council responded to popular pressure by introducing change while skilfully heading off Habsburg anger. So German city rulers often took risks in introducing religious change, and sometimes the calculation of risk outweighed any decision to reform: in the cases of Augsburg and Cologne, commerical and political considerations eventually decided, or forced, the cities to avoid, or severely restrict, religious alteration.

When German cities – not only the free imperial cities but cities that were part of states, such as Luther's university town of Erfurt – did accept the reform they, and their rulers in particular, were likely to be influenced by the following thoughts: the need to maintain consensus in the urban community and avert disorder by bringing in gradual and moderate religious change; and the possibilities of renewing urban society, of promoting education, morality and poor relief through the new priorities of the Evangelical faith. It should also be said that the German cities – typically proud of their independence – sometimes adopted the Reformation in a form (not always an orthodox Lutheran form) appropriate to their circumstances and outlook, often synthesizing various influences. Thus the Reformation in Strassburg, under the leadership of Martin Bucer (1491–1551), combined tendencies from Lutheranism with others from the Reformation implemented by Ulrich Zwingli (1484–1531) in the Swiss city of Zürich. The Strassburg civic model of Reformation was widely emulated in the cities of the German south and south-west.

The genuine Lutheran piety that affected the leaders of German urban society in adopting the Reformation also motivated the princely rulers of many German territorial states. Such rulers had an important part to play in implementing and protecting the Lutheran Reformation after its initial, and largely urban phase was over. A good example of a pious German Evangelical prince was Luther's ruler in succession to Frederick the Wise, John, styled the Steadfast. Luther much admired John and had for him none of the ambiguous feelings he had had for Frederick. In truth, John was an unswerving Lutheran prince and under his auspices, after his accession in 1525, Electoral Saxony became, as Luther commented in 1530, the model Evangelical polity; its Visitation system, designed to put the reform into practical effect in the parishes, was set up by John in 1527 with the direct participation of Luther and Melanchthon.

As part and parcel of the reform in those German territories that went over to the Reformation in the 1520s and 30s – states such as Anhalt, Brunswick (Braunschweig), Prussia, Electoral and ducal Saxony, Württemberg and Hesse – considerable amounts of Church property, especially that of the monks, changed hands and fell to the princes to administer. Was it a motive in declaring for the Reformation that property would in this way accrue to princes and enrich them? Luther felt that this *was* a motive with some (unnamed) princes, but if we look at the actual outcome in two of the most important German Lutheran states, Hesse and Electoral Saxony, we find that the personal self-enrichment of princes can hardly have been a dominant motive, since in these states confiscated Church wealth went, as the Lutheran ideal said it should, to schooling, parsons' wages, poor relief, hospitals and a university. Neither can we say that, in espousing the Reformation, the typical German Lutheran prince was intending simply to defy the Holy Roman Emperor or to expand his regional power by choosing a religion different from that of the Catholic

47

Habsburg overlord. At the end of the day, despite the tension between the princely and imperial poles of attraction, it was not in the interest of rulers to demolish the principle of *Obrigkeit* – authority – on which their own positions, no less than that of their suzerain, the *Kaiser*, rested. Nor would anyone in Germany in the 1520s, 1530s or 1540s lightheartedly challenge the position of Charles V, a world monarch whose power and reputation increased by the year. The challenge came, but one motive underlying it was a serious sense on the part of leading German Lutheran princes that they must answer to God for the spiritual welfare of their subjects, and that therefore they might even have to take issue with the mighty emperor himself if he bade them renounce their Evangelical allegiance.

Such decisions had to be taken in and after 1530. The year closed a decade in which the Lutheran faith had emerged as the most important moderate progressive force in German social and religious life. Many who had rallied to Luther as an anti-clerical or national champion, or simply as a rebel, perhaps drifted away as his protest hardened out into an organized creed. The peasants, in so far as they had been spontaneous adherents of the Lutheran cause, may have been lost after 1525. Perhaps they simply and passively followed their princes' inclinations; perhaps many of them were attracted by the new forms of religious radicalism, especially Anabaptism, that grew up on the left of the Zwinglian and Lutheran Reformations in Switzerland and Germany in the 1520s. The Christian humanists, led by Erasmus, had rallied to Luther because his protests against religious superstition and corruption seemed to be the same as their own; however, in 1524 and 1525 Luther and Erasmus waged a literary war over the question of man's free will, and the opposition between the two men – Luther insisting that man's will was shackled – became complete. The foremost leader of the Protestant Reformation in Switzerland, Ulrich Zwingli, was in some ways a disciple of Erasmus. Luther took violently against him in a disagreement over whether Christ was bodily present in Holy Communion, with Luther arguing forcibly against Zwingli that He was. Not only was the emergent Protestant Reformation divided from other schools of opinion, such as the Erasmian Christian humanists, the

Anabaptists of the 'Radical Reformation' and the Catholic mainstream; in addition, divisions opened up and multiplied within the Protestant Reformation as variants – Zwinglian, Bucerian and, later, Calvinist, appeared; there were even discords within the Lutheran camp: for example, one of Luther's disciples, Johann Agricola (1499–1566) taught, in what to Luther was an unacceptably extreme form, Luther's own doctrine that the justified Christian was set free from the law.

The divisions in the Reformation just described were all the more dangerous to Protestantism inasmuch as the Catholic cause was rapidly regaining confidence – if only, as yet, on the political front. In 1529 the Catholic-dominated *Reichstag* at Speyer passed a law ruling out toleration and reaffirming the 1521 Edict of Worms. A vocal minority of Lutheran members of the *Reichstag* entered a protest (the famous protest that gives us the word Protestant) against this outcome, but in the following year Emperor Charles V returned to Germany to deal in person with the religious issue. The year 1530 marked a high point in Charles's career: he had secured his position in Italy, established his political mastery over the papacy, come to terms with France and was able, for the moment, to hold the Turks at bay. His formal coronation as Holy Roman Emperor by Pope Clement VII was a fitting recognition of his imposing power in Europe. When he convened the *Reichstag* to Augsburg in 1530, he was clearly confident of his ability to solve this outstanding problem of Martin Luther.

Luther himself, as an outlaw, was not to attend the *Reichstag*. His aide, Philip Melanchthon, went instead and submitted a lengthy summary of the Lutheran faith, the Augsburg Confession. The *Reichstag* rejected this confession and, restating earlier decisions against the Lutherans, gave them a brief period in which to conform to Catholicism. In reply, a group of Lutheran estates of the *Reichstag*, meeting in the town of Schmalkalden in February 1531, formed a defensive association, the Schmalkaldic League. The formation of this league could easily have been construed as an act of rebellion in itself, and hence banned by Luther's own political writings against active resistance to authority. However, in his 1531 tract, *Dr Martin Luther's Warning to his Dear German People*, Luther argued that there was a right of

49

defensive resistance for religious causes, and that the proper people to exercise it were the territorial princes.

With the formation of the Schmalkaldic League, religious tension increased in Germany. The following factors helped to avert a head-on clash and a civil war between Catholic and Protestant sides: first, basic patriotism, and personal loyalty towards the emperor (which Luther shared); second, a feeling of danger from the Turks, who were believed to be poised to invade Europe, and Germany in particular, so that it was thought necessary for Germans to be united, rather than divided by religion; third, a continued search for the restoration of religious unity by peaceful means, evidenced in periodic conferences, such as the talks at Ratisbon (Regensburg) in 1541 between theologians entrusted with working out a formula of agreement between the two Christian faiths. For all these reasons, the civil war that the formation of the Schmalkaldic League might have provoked was avoided and religious peace was restored with the Truce of Nürnberg in 1532.

Despite this, numerous individual incidents showed how rife tension was in Germany in the last two decades of Luther's life. People were anxiously watching for gains to one side or the other as a measure of the strength of each party. In part, the tension came about because the rivalries of German princes got caught up in the religious strife. One area of friction waa the southern ducal state of Württemberg. Here, in 1534, the Schmalkaldic League restored the Protestant duke Ulrich to his dukedom. Another success for the Lutherans, where they acquired extensive territorial gains through a partly political decision, was in the state of Brunswick, where the aggressive Catholic duke, Henry, whom Luther regarded as a particular foe, was deposed by a Protestant coalition and the Lutheran religion introduced. The Reformation was also adopted in key bishoprics, notably Naumburg in Saxony and Archbishop von Hohenzollern's base at Halle. The success of the Evangelical cause was, however, also sometimes impeded by the ambitions and faults of individual Lutheran princes. After the death in 1539 of the Catholic Duke George of Saxony, the Protestant faith was brought in, but a new duke in the 1540s weakened the cause in the heartland of German

Lutheranism by quarrelling over territory with his cousin, John, Elector of Saxony. There was also a weakness in the leading figure of the Schmalkaldic League, the once-ferocious Lutheran campaigner, Philip of Hesse. In 1540 Philip arranged a bigamous marriage for himself, sanctioned, most unwisely, by Luther and Melanchthon. Bigamy was a capital offence in Germany, and this fact gave Charles V a hold over the leading light in the Schmalkaldic League. As a virtual agent of the emperor, Philip of Hesse helped to prevent the Protestant alliance from attaining anything like maximum membership or effectiveness for much of the 1540s.

Germany, until after Luther's death, lived through a precarious religious peace. Luther himself was not at peace in these years. In the 1530s and 1540s, when he was in his forties, fifties and early sixties, Luther wrote and spoke as if he were a very old man. This was partly the convention of the age, as were his often reiterated wishes for death and his desire for martyrdom. It is true that Luther's health was exceedingly bad for much of the time during these years. He would write to his friends in great detail about his aches and pains and his various bodily emissions. But despite his habitual hypochondria, he was often in genuinely great pain, above all with the appalling kidney complaint known as the stone. Perhaps this pain increased the irritability that we see in his last years. In addition, there were recurrences of the old depressiveness, especially as he contemplated a Germany whose moral faults his Reformation had not reformed and a Christendom to whose unity he had brought schism. His greatest failure – the other architects of the Lutheran Church seem hardly to have been conscious of it as failure – was his inability to bring the whole of Christendom over to his reform of what he had hoped to hold together as a united and Catholic Church, minus the pope. In the mid-1540s the papacy was far from vanquished and was, in fact, preparing a great council that was to reform the Roman Catholic Church. Luther's anger against his old enemy, the papacy, was expressed with unprecedented force in his *Against the Papacy at Rome, founded by the Devil*. With its curse of syphilis and other ills on the 'Sodomite Pope', this pamphlet makes bitter reading, as does Luther's intensely disagreeable pamphlet of 1543 against the

Jews. Inexcusable as it is, Luther's anti-semitic writing reflects his disappointments in his late years – disappointment, in this case, of an earlier hope that his reform of the Church would necessarily convert the Jews to Christ.

Despite bitterness and unhappiness, the aging Luther had consolations. He was certainly the most famous religious leader of the era. He was consulted on several German issues – although he was generally naïve on political questions and his advice, as in the affair of Philip of Hesse's bigamy, could be seriously misguided. Nevertheless his fellow Germans had the greatest respect for him as a counsellor: his death in 1546 was brought on by his travelling, while gravely ill, to sort out a quarrel between the counts of Mansfeld.

Besides the consolations that came from the esteem in which he was held, Luther enjoyed domestic comforts and family life after his marriage in 1525 to an ex-nun, Katherine von Bora. Katherine came from a vaguely noble background, and she was mean, careful and a good manager – all the things that her husband was not. Luther treated her in an affectionate, patronizing and teasing way. There were children, to whom Luther behaved in a quite different way from the brutalities of his own parents towards him. At the Luther home there was also a floating population of students boarders and other house guests, some of whom started the habit of jotting down Luther's dinner-table conversations, or monologues, later published as his 'Table Talk'. These suppertime chats, like so many of his writings, reveal Luther: impulsive, open, warm, overpowering, spontaneous, heavily humorous, clearly tipsy sometimes, prejudiced, conservative, childishly ignorant and superstitious on many matters, as credulous as any peasant, yet deeply learned in his field and an undoubted religious genius. After his death Germany fell apart in a religious civil war and Luther's own Evangelical movement split in bitter theological rivalry between his followers. In many ways a destructive force, he was also seized by a vital and valid religious insight, supported by an extraordinary personal courage. As far as any one man can be responsible for a great movement, Martin Luther was responsible for the Lutheran Reformation.

Bibliography

Place of publication is London unless otherwise stated.

The bibliography is divided into general background works, and works on Luther and the German Reformation in particular.

G. R. Potter and Denys Hay (eds), *The New Cambridge Modern History, Volume I: The Renaissance* (Cambridge, U. P., 1961) has useful chapters on the state of the Church, the Renaissance and Germany 1493–1519. G. R. Elton (ed.), *The New Cambridge Modern History, Volume II: The Reformation* (Cambridge, U. P., 1962) is probably still the best single-volume survey in English of Reformation Europe (note especially Chapter III). A. G. Dickens, *The Age of Humanism and Reformation. Europe in the Fourteenth, Fifteenth and Sixteenth Centuries* (Englewood Cliffs, N.J., Prentice-Hall, 1977) provides an excellent condensed survey of the pre-Reformation and Reformation periods. Professor Dickens's *Reformation and Society in Sixteenth-Century Europe* (Thames & Hudson, 1966) is a lavishly illustrated introduction. G. R. Elton, *Reformation Europe 1517–1559* (Fontana, 1967) takes as its focus Europe in the age of Charles V.

Students wishing to read something of Luther himself should use Ian D. Kingston Siggins, *Luther* (Edinburgh, Oliver & Boyd, 1972) or Benjamin Drewery and E. G. Rupp, *Martin Luther* (Edward Arnold, 1970). Edited by H. G. Koenigsberger, *Luther. A Profile* (Macmillan, 1973) is a valuable collection of essays from various vantage points, including the Marxist and the 'psycho-historical'. There is more of the latter in a book mentioned in the text of this pamphlet, Erik H. Erikson, *Young Man Luther. A Study in Psychoanalysis and History* (Faber & Faber, 1958). Roland H. Bainton, *Here I Stand. A Life of Martin*

Luther (Hodder & Stoughton, 1951) is lively, and unashamedly hero-worshipping. Gerhard Ritter, *Luther. His Life and Work* (trans. John Riches, Collins, 1963) provides a fine standard biography. For an intelligible guide to Luther's theology and its development, see Gordon Rupp, *The Righteousness of God. Luther Studies* (Hodder & Stoughton, 1963). A. G. Dickens, *The German Nation and Martin Luther* (Edward Arnold, 1974) ably summarizes the results of much detailed research. He emphasizes the theme of the urban Reformation, a subject also thoroughly explored in Steven E. Ozment, *The Reformation in the Cities. The Appeal of Protestantism to Sixteenth-Century Germany and Switzerland* (New Haven, Yale University Press, 1975) and in Bernd Moeller, *Imperial Cities and the Reformation* (Fortress, Philadelphia, 1972). A massive study of Luther, to 1521, is Robert Herndon Fife, *The Revolt of Martin Luther* (New York, Columbia U. P., 1968). James Atkinson, *Martin Luther and the Birth of Protestantism* (Marshall Morgan & Scott, 1968) is readable, authoritative and sympathetic.